Overcoming Arthritis

Overcoming Arthritis

Ms. Sudesta

Library of Congress Control Number: 2007901308
ISBN: Hardcover   978-1-4257-5693-2
                   Softcover   978-1-4257-5691-8

To order additional copies of this book, contact:
Xlibris Corporation
1-888-795-4274
www.Xlibris.com
Orders@Xlibris.com
34370

CONTENTS

DEDICATION

This book is dedicated to My Family, Friends,
and all Who Suffer from Arthritis

Acknowledgments

I thank God for all scripture given. Thank you to my mother and my husband who encouraged me to write. Thanks to the Arthritis Foundation for compelling me to write. A final thank you to the National Institute of Arthritis and Musculoskeletal and Skin Diseases (NIAMS) for encouraging readers to duplicate and distribute copies of NIH Publication No. 02-4999.

A gift for:

From:

A Rainbow

A rainbow is a
Token of the covenant
Between God and me

Sudesta

Sudesta's Story

"I AM AN ARTHRITIS OVERCOMER."

I was diagnosed with arthritis as a child. It was really hard for me to be active as a child and later as a teenager due to my arthritis condition. As a teenager I remember having recurring pain, stiffness, and swelling in my legs. My mother took me to our family doctor. He examined me and told her my symptoms were caused by arthritis. During the visit, she did not think to ask questions to learn more about my arthritis condition. The doctor prescribed pain medication and sent us home.

Later as an adult, I experienced recurring pain, stiffness, and swelling in my ankles, back, elbows, feet, fingers, hip, knees, legs, neck, toes, and wrists. I saw a doctor at my HMO. She told me my symptoms were caused by arthritis. She prescribed pain medication but this time I asked questions. Over the years, I educated myself about my arthritis condition. I learned that prescription and over-the-counter medications are the traditional treatment for arthritis.

The most important thing to know about arthritis medications is the possible side effects. Side effects are generally divided into 4 categories—those that are common, less common, most common, and rare. Patients are usually given information about the most common side effects. In my case, I must know the side effects in all 4 categories.

Many prescription and over-the-counter drugs contain dyes (i.e. black, blue, brown, green, orange, pink, purple, red, yellow, etc.) that can cause allergic reactions in some people. I have experienced *less common* side effects when taking drugs containing dyes. Specifically, some of *the less common* side effects I have experienced depending on the type of drug are: abdominal pain, back pain, confusion, constipation, fluid retention, gas, heart palpitations, muscle cramps and spasms, nausea, nervousness, rashes, severe joint pain, stiffness, and swelling in the legs or arms, etc. I do not take any medications with these side effects, and I have not had any of these symptoms in years.

I have learned things (i.e. allergies, clothing, cosmetics, drinks, drugs, food, multiple chemical sensitivities, etc.), can provoke arthritis symptoms in some people. Part One, explains how abstaining from specific things has helped me to control my arthritis symptoms. Part Two, explains how benefiting from specific things has provided me immediate and perhaps permanent relief from my arthritis symptoms.

"YOU CAN BE AN ARTHRITIS OVERCOMER TOO!"

Becoming Self-Aware

These questions are provided to help individuals decide if he or she might have an arthritis condition provoked by things (i.e. allergies, clothing, cosmetics, drinks, drugs, foods, multiple chemical sensitivities, etc.).

TWENTY QUESTIONS

1. Are your utilities electric, gas, or oil?
2. Does your furnace have a removable or washable filter?
3. Do you crave foods like chocolate?
4. Do you drink alcohol?
5. Do you eat (i.e. beef, butter, cheese, coffee, corn, cured meats, eggs, grapefruit, lamb, lemon, milk, oats, oranges, peanuts, pork, sugar, wheat, etc.) 3 to 6 times per week?
6. Do you have allergies or asthma?
7. Do you have gout?
8. Do you have multiple chemical sensitivities?
9. Do you have rheumatoid arthritis?
10. Do you have sleep apnea?
11. Do you have wall-to-wall carpet or area rugs?
12. Do you live in an apartment or townhouse?
13. Do you sleep on down, feather, foam, or polyester pillows?
14. Do you sleep on a foam or wool mattress?
15. Do you smoke or live with a smoker?
16. Do you take any prescribed, non-prescribed or natural drugs containing dyes (i.e. black, blue, brown, green, orange, pink, purple, red, yellow, etc.) or mold?

17. Do you use dye containing (i.e. black, blue, brown, etc.) clothing, cosmetics, drinks, drugs, food, etc.?
18. Do you use products made of synthetic fabrics (i.e. acrylic, nylon, or polyester)?
19. Do you use scented products?
20. Have you had any chemical exposures either frequent, one large exposure or small exposures?

If you answered yes to several questions, call your doctor. Take the list to show the doctor. You may need to see a Board Certified Allergist to find out if you have allergies and/or multiple chemical sensitivities.

All Scripture Given

But continue thou in the things which thou hast learned and hast been assured of, knowing of whom thou hast learned them; And that from a child thou hast known the holy scriptures, which are able to make thee wise unto salvation through faith which is in Christ Jesus. All scripture is given by inspiration of God, and is profitable for doctrine, for reproof, for correction, for instruction in righteousness: That the man of God may be perfect, throughly furnished unto all good works. (2 Timothy 3:14-17).

PART ONE

Abstaining from Things

Abstain from all appearance of evil. And the very God of peace sanctify you wholly; and I pray God your whole spirit and soul and body be preserved blameless unto the coming of our Lord Jesus Christ. Faithful is he that calleth you, who also will do it. Brethren, pray for us. Greet all the brethren with an holy kiss. I charge you by the Lord that this epistle be read unto all the holy brethren. The grace of our Lord Jesus Christ be with you. Amen. (1 Thessalonians 5:22-28).

1

Alcohol

DON'T DRINK ALCOHOL UNLESS YOU KNOW IT IS SAFE. Does alcohol provoke your arthritis symptoms? If you don't know, give up alcohol (i.e. beer, liquor, wine) for two weeks and see if your symptoms are better or worst. Drinking too much alcohol can cause gout. Any drinks, drugs, food, etc. containing alcohol can interfere with the elimination of uric acid.

2

Aluminum

DON'T USE ALUMINUM UNLESS YOU KNOW IT IS SAFE. Does aluminum provoke your arthritis symptoms? If you don't know, give up aluminum (i.e. aluminum is found in some antacids, antiperspirant deodorants, baking powder, containers, cookware, foil, toothpaste, water, etc.) for two weeks and see if your symptoms are better or worst.

3

Artificial Lighting

DON'T USE ARTIFICIAL LIGHTING UNLESS YOU KNOW IT IS SAFE. Does artificial lighting provoke your arthritis symptoms? If you don't know, give up artificial lighting (i.e. lack of natural light, use of tinted glasses and contacts, fluorescents) as much as possible and see if your symptoms are better or worst.

4

Bathing

DON'T BATHE UNLESS YOU KNOW IT IS SAFE. Does bathing provoke your arthritis symptoms? If you don't know, try bathing (i.e. baths and showers) at night for two weeks and see if your symptoms are better or worst.

5

Beef

DON'T EAT BEEF UNLESS YOU KNOW IT IS SAFE. Does beef provoke your arthritis symptoms? If you don't know, give up beef for two weeks and see if your symptoms are better or worst.

6

Butter

DON'T EAT BUTTER UNLESS YOU KNOW IT IS SAFE. Does butter provoke your arthritis symptoms? If you don't know, give up butter for two weeks and see if your symptoms are better or worst.

7

Caffeine

DON'T DRINK CAFFEINE PRODUCTS UNLESS YOU KNOW IT IS SAFE. Does caffeine provoke your arthritis symptoms? If you don't know, give up caffeine (i.e. chocolate, coffee, colas, some pain relievers, tea, etc.) for two weeks and see if your symptoms are better or worst.

8

Cereal

DON'T EAT CEREAL UNLESS YOU KNOW IT IS SAFE. Does cereal provoke your arthritis symptoms? If you don't know, give up cereal (i.e. cereal containing corn and wheat) for two weeks and see if your symptoms are better or worst.

9

Cheese

DON'T EAT CHEESE UNLESS YOU KNOW IT IS SAFE. Does cheese provoke your arthritis symptoms? If you don't know, give up cheese for two weeks and see if your symptoms are better or worst.

10

Chemical Additives

DON'T EAT CHEMICAL ADDITIVES UNLESS YOU KNOW IT IS SAFE. Do chemical additives provoke your arthritis symptoms? If you don't know, give up chemical additives (i.e. artificial colorings, which have been shown to cause allergic reactions and other health problems, aspartame, BHA (butylated hydroxyanisole), BHT (butylated hydroxytoluene), Blue Dye, fructose, glycerides, MSG (monosodium glutamate), nitrites and nitrates sodium, Red Dye, Yellow Dye, saccharin, sulphur dioxide, etc.) for two weeks and see if your symptoms are better or worst. I always read labels to determine if any of these chemical additives are used in cosmetics, drinks, drugs or food that I buy.

11

Chemical Fumes

DON'T BE EXPOSED TO CHEMICAL FUMES UNLESS YOU KNOW IT IS SAFE. Do chemical fumes provoke your arthritis symptoms? If you don't know, avoid chemical fumes (i.e. new carpet, new cars, new furniture, new homes, newsprint, paint, solvents, etc.) for two weeks and see if your symptoms are better or worst.

12

Corn

DON'T EAT CORN UNLESS YOU KNOW IT IS SAFE. Does corn provoke your arthritis symptoms? If you don't know, give up corn (i.e. drinks and food containing corn) for two weeks and see if your symptoms are better or worst.

13

Craved Foods

DON'T EAT CRAVED FOODS UNLESS YOU KNOW IT IS SAFE. Do craved foods provoke your arthritis symptoms? If you don't know, give up craved foods (i.e. any food which you crave or which triggers eating binges) for two weeks and see if your symptoms are better or worst.

14

Dried Fruits

DON'T EAT DRIED FRUITS UNLESS YOU KNOW IT IS SAFE. Do dried fruits provoke your arthritis symptoms? If you don't know, give up dried fruits (i.e. commercially dried fruits and raisins) for two weeks and see if your symptoms are better or worst.

15

Drugs

DON'T USE PRESCRIPTION OR OVER-THE-COUNTER DRUGS UNLESS YOU KNOW IT IS SAFE. Do you use drugs that provoke your arthritis symptoms? If you don't know, you should find out if the drugs' possible side effects include: joint inflammation or pains, muscle cramps, spasms, and stiffness, etc.).

16

Dyes

DON'T USE DYES UNLESS YOU KNOW IT IS SAFE. Do products containing dyes provoke your arthritis symptoms? If you don't know, give up products (i.e. clothing, cosmetics, drinks, drugs, food, etc.) containing dyes for two weeks and see if your symptoms are better or worst.

17

Eggs

DON'T EAT EGGS UNLESS YOU KNOW IT IS SAFE. Do eggs provoke your arthritis symptoms? If you don't know, give up eggs for two weeks and see if your symptoms are better or worst.

18

Engine Exhaust Fumes

DON'T BREATHE ENGINE EXHAUST FUMES UNLESS YOU KNOW
IT IS SAFE. Does breathing engine exhaust fumes provoke your arthritis
symptoms? If you don't know, wear a mask when driving or when outside
for two weeks and see if your symptoms are better or worst.

19

Factory Foods

DON'T USE FACTORY FOODS UNLESS YOU KNOW IT IS SAFE. Do factory foods provoke your arthritis symptoms? If you don't know, give up factory foods (i.e. processed and canned foods) for two weeks and see if your symptoms are better or worst.

20

Fried Foods

DON'T EAT FRIED FOODS UNLESS YOU KNOW IT IS SAFE. Does fried food provoke your arthritis symptoms? If you don't know, give up fried foods (i.e. foods fried in any kind of oil or fat) for two weeks and see if your symptoms are better or worst.

21

Grapefruits

DON'T EAT GRAPEFRUITS UNLESS YOU KNOW IT IS SAFE. Do grapefruits provoke your arthritis symptoms? If you don't know, give up grapefruits (i.e. juice, etc.) for two weeks and see if your symptoms are better or worst.

22

Household Cleaners

DON'T USE HOUSEHOLD CLEANERS UNLESS YOU KNOW IT IS SAFE. Do household cleaners provoke your arthritis symptoms? If you don't know, give up household cleaners (i.e. toxic cleaners, and disinfectants, etc.) for two weeks and see if your symptoms are better or worst. Baking soda, borax, salt, or vinegar mixed with water are nontoxic alternatives.

23

Hydrogenated Oils

DON'T USE HYDROGENATED OILS UNLESS YOU KNOW IT IS SAFE. Do hydrogenated oils provoke your arthritis symptoms? If you don't know, give up hydrogenated oils (i.e. all margarines, all partially hydrogenated oils) for two weeks and see if your symptoms are better or worst.

24

Incense

DON'T USE INCENSE UNLESS YOU KNOW IT IS SAFE. Does burning incense provoke your arthritis symptoms? If you don't know, give up burning incense for two weeks and see if your symptoms are better or worst.

25

Lamb

DON'T EAT LAMB UNLESS YOU KNOW IT IS SAFE. Does lamb provoke your arthritis symptoms? If you don't know, give up lamb for two weeks and see if your symptoms are better or worst.

26

Lemons

DON'T EAT LEMONS UNLESS YOU KNOW IT IS SAFE. Do lemons provoke your arthritis symptoms? If you don't know, give up lemons (i.e. juice, etc.) for two weeks and see if your symptoms are better or worst.

27

Malt

DON'T EAT MALT UNLESS YOU KNOW IT IS SAFE. Does malt provoke your arthritis symptoms? If you don't know, give up malt for two weeks and see if your symptoms are better or worst.

28

Mattresses

DON'T USE MATTRESSES UNLESS YOU KNOW IT IS SAFE. Do mattresses provoke your arthritis symptoms? If you don't know, give up mattresses (i.e. foam or wool) for two weeks and see if your symptoms are better or worst. Try using an air mattress.

29

Meats

DON'T EAT MEATS UNLESS YOU KNOW IT IS SAFE. Do meats provoke your arthritis symptoms? If you don't know, give up cured meats (i.e. bacon, bologna, canned meats, cold cuts, ham, hot dogs, luncheon meats, etc.) for two weeks and see if your symptoms are better or worst.

30

Milk

DON'T DRINK MILK UNLESS YOU KNOW IT IS SAFE. Does milk
provoke your arthritis symptoms? If you don't know, give up milk and milk
products for two weeks and see if your symptoms are better or worst.

31

Mold

DON'T EAT MOLD-TAINTED FOOD UNLESS YOU KNOW IT IS
SAFE. Does mold-tainted food provoke your arthritis symptoms? If you
don't know, do not eat mold-tainted food (i.e. bread, etc.) for two weeks
and see if your symptoms are better or worst.

32

Mothballs

DON'T USE MOTHBALLS UNLESS YOU KNOW IT IS SAFE. Do mothballs provoke your arthritis symptoms? If you don't know, give up mothballs for two weeks and see if your symptoms are better or worst.

33

Oats

DON'T EAT OATS UNLESS YOU KNOW IT IS SAFE. Do oats provoke your arthritis symptoms? If you don't know, give up oats (i.e. bread, oatmeal, etc.) for two weeks and see if your symptoms are better or worst.

34

Oranges

DON'T EAT ORANGES UNLESS YOU KNOW IT IS SAFE. Do oranges provoke your arthritis symptoms? If you don't know, give up oranges (i.e. juice, etc.) for two weeks and see if your symptoms are better or worst.

35

Peanuts

DON'T EAT PEANUTS UNLESS YOU KNOW IT IS SAFE. Do peanuts provoke your arthritis symptoms? If you don't know, give up peanuts (i.e. candy, cookies, ice cream, etc.) for two weeks and see if your symptoms are better or worst.

36

Pillows

DON'T USE PILLOWS UNLESS YOU KNOW IT IS SAFE. Do your pillows provoke your arthritis symptoms? If you don't know, give up pillows (i.e. feathered, form or polyester pillows, etc.) for two weeks and see if your symptoms are better or worst. I use white cotton pillows and white cotton pillowcases.

37

Pork

DON'T EAT PORK UNLESS YOU KNOW IT IS SAFE. Does pork provoke your arthritis symptoms? If you don't know, give up pork for two weeks and see if your symptoms are better or worst.

38

Reactive Foods

DON'T EAT REACTIVE FOODS UNLESS YOU KNOW IT IS SAFE. Do reactive foods provoke your arthritis symptoms? If you don't know, give up reactive foods (i.e. any foods known to cause allergic or allergic-like reactions) for two weeks and see if your symptoms are better or worst.

39

Refined Foods

DON'T EAT REFINED FOODS UNLESS YOU KNOW IT IS SAFE. Do refined foods provoke your arthritis symptoms? If you don't know, give up refined foods (i.e. white flour products, etc.) for two weeks and see if your symptoms are better or worst.

40

Rye

DON'T EAT RYE UNLESS YOU KNOW IT IS SAFE. Does rye provoke your arthritis symptoms? If you don't know, give up rye for two weeks and see if your symptoms are better or worst.

41

Scented Products

DON'T USE SCENTED PRODUCTS UNLESS YOU KNOW IT SAFE. Do scented products provoke your arthritis symptoms? If you don't know, give up scented products (colognes, cosmetics, deodorants, lotions, perfumes, soaps, etc.) for two weeks and see if your symptoms are better or worst.

42

Soap

DON'T USE SOAP UNLESS YOU KNOW IT IS SAFE. Does soap
provoke your arthritis symptoms? If you don't know, give up soap (i.e. bar
soap, detergent, dish soap, liquid soap, etc.) for two weeks and see if your
symptoms are better or worst. Try using dye-free, unscented, soap-free,
hypo-allergenic and dermatologist tested products.

43

Sodas

DON'T DRINK SODAS UNLESS YOU KNOW IT IS SAFE. Do sodas provoke your arthritis symptoms? If you don't know, give up sodas (i.e. diet and regular) for two weeks and see if your symptoms are better or worst.

44

Sodium

DON'T USE SODIUM UNLESS YOU KNOW IT IS SAFE. Does sodium provoke your arthritis symptoms? If you don't know, give up sodium (i.e. additives and added salt to foods and beverages including bottled water containing sodium) two weeks and see if your symptoms are better or worst.

45

Soy

DON'T EAT SOY UNLESS YOU KNOW IT IS SAFE. Does soy provoke your arthritis symptoms? If you don't know, give up soy (i.e. drinks, foods, etc.) for two weeks and see if your symptoms are better or worst.

46

Stairs

DON'T USE THE STAIRS UNLESS YOU KNOW IT IS SAFE. Does walking up and down stairs provoke your arthritis symptoms? If you don't know, give up walking up and down stairs as much as possible for two weeks and see if your symptoms are better or worst.

47

Sugar

DON'T USE SUGAR UNLESS YOU KNOW IT IS SAFE. Does sugar provoke your arthritis symptoms? If you don't know, give up sugar in all forms for two weeks and see if your symptoms are better or worst.

48

Synthetic Fabrics

DON'T USE SYNTHETIC FABRICS UNLESS YOU KNOW IT IS SAFE.
Do synthetic fabrics provoke your arthritis symptoms? If you don't know,
give up synthetic fabrics (i.e. acrylic, nylon, polyester, etc.) for two weeks
and see if your symptoms are better or worst.

49

Tobacco Smoke

DON'T USE TOBACCO PRODUCTS UNLESS YOU KNOW IT IS SAFE. Do tobacco products provoke your arthritis symptoms? If you don't know, give up tobacco products (i.e. direct or indirect) for two weeks and see if your symptoms are better or worst.

50

Tomatoes

DON'T EAT TOMATOES UNLESS YOU KNOW IT IS SAFE. Do tomatoes provoke your arthritis symptoms? If you don't know, give up tomatoes (i.e. juice, etc.) for two weeks and see if your symptoms are better or worst.

51

Water

DON'T DRINK WATER UNLESS YOU KNOW IT IS SAFE. Does water provoke your arthritis symptoms? If you don't know, give up water (i.e. bottled water containing sodium, spring, tap, etc.) for two weeks and see if your symptoms are better or worst.

52

Wheat

DON'T EAT WHEAT UNLESS YOU KNOW IT IS SAFE. Does wheat provoke your arthritis symptoms? If you don't know, give up wheat (i.e. bread, crackers, etc.) for two weeks and see if your symptoms are better or worst.

PART TWO

Benefiting from Things

Bless the LORD, O my soul: and all that is within me, bless his holy name. Bless the LORD, O my soul, and forget not all his benefits: Who forgiveth all thine iniquities; who healeth all thy diseases; Who redeemeth thy life from destruction; who crowneth thee with lovingkindness and tender mercies; Who satisfieth thy mouth with good things; so that thy youth is renewed like the eagle's. (Psalm 103:1-5).

53

Activities

BENEFIT FROM ACTIVITIES. Studies show that an estimated 18 percent of Americans who have arthritis or other rheumatic conditions believe that their condition limits their activities. People with arthritis may find that they can no longer participate in some of their favorite activities, which can affect their overall well-being. Even when arthritis impairs only one joint, a person may have to change many daily activities to protect that joint from further damage and reduce pain. When arthritis affects the entire body, as it does in people with rheumatoid arthritis or fibromyalgia, many daily activities have to be changed to deal with pain, fatigue, and other symptoms (NIH Publication No. 02-4999).

54

Assistive Devices

BENEFIT FROM ASSISTIVE DEVICES. The most common assistive devices for treating arthritis pain are splints and braces, which are used to support weakened joints or allow them to rest. Some of these devices prevent the joint from moving; others allow some movement. A splint or brace should be used only when recommended by a doctor or therapist, who will show the patient the correct way to put the device on, ensure that it fits properly, and explain when and for how long it should be worn. The incorrect use of a splint or brace can cause joint damage, stiffness, and pain.

A person with arthritis can use other kinds of devices to ease the pain. For example, the use of a cane when walking can reduce some of the weight placed on a knee or hip affected by arthritis. A shoe insert (orthotic) can ease the pain of walking caused by arthritis of the foot or knee. Other devices can help with activities such as opening jars, closing zippers, and holding pencils (NIH Publication No. 02-4999).

55

Capsaicin Cream

BENEFIT FROM CAPSAICIN CREAM. Capsaicin cream is a preparation put on the skin to relieve joint or muscle pain when only one or two joints are involved (NIH Publication No. 02-4999). Does capsaicin cream relieve your arthritis symptoms? If you don't know, you should talk to your doctor before using capsaicin cream.

56

Chiropractic Therapy

BENEFIT FROM CHIROPRACTIC THERAPY. Chiropractic therapy is a natural method of healing, advocating a drugless, non-invasive, and non-surgical treatment that can result in reduced pain and inflammation. Does chiropractic therapy relieve your arthritis symptoms? If you don't know, you should talk to your doctor before using chiropractic therapy.

57

Cold Therapy

BENEFIT FROM COLD THERAPY. Cold therapy numbs the nerves around the joint (which reduces pain) and may relieve inflammation and muscle spasms. Cold therapy can involve cold packs, ice massage, soaking in cold water, or over-the counter sprays and ointments that cool the skin and joints (NIH Publication No. 02-4999). Does cold therapy relieve your arthritis symptoms? If you don't know, you should talk to your doctor before using cold therapy.

58

Cotton

BENEFIT FROM USING COTTON. 100% Cotton dye-free fabrics (i.e. clothing, mattresses, pillows, rugs, sheets, towels, etc.) can provide comfort and relief to people who suffer from arthritis. Does using cotton dye-free fabrics relieve your arthritis symptoms? If you don't know, try using cotton dye-free fabrics for two weeks and see if your symptoms are better or worst.

59

Devices Used in Treatment

BENEFIT FROM DEVICES USED IN TREATMENT. Transcutaneous electrical nerve stimulation (TENS) has been found effective in modifying pain perception. TENS blocks pain messages to the brain with a small device that directs mild electric pulses to nerve endings that lie beneath the painful area of the skin.

A blood-filtering device called the Prosorba Column is used in some health care facilities for filtering out harmful antibodies in people with severe rheumatoid arthritis (NIH Publication No. 02-4999).

60

Diagnosis

BENEFIT FROM DIAGNOSIS. Diagnosing rheumatic diseases can be difficult because some symptoms and signs are common to many different diseases. A general practitioner or family doctor may be able to evaluate a patient or refer him or her to a rheumatologist (a doctor who specializes in treating arthritis and other rheumatic diseases).

The doctor will review the patient's medical history, conduct a physical examination, and obtain laboratory tests and x-rays or other imaging tests. The doctor may need to see the patient more than once to make an accurate diagnosis (NIH Publication No. 02-4999).

61

Diet Therapy

BENEFIT FROM DIET THERAPY. Another important part of a treatment program is a well-balanced diet. Along with exercise, a well-balanced diet helps people manage their body weight and stay healthy. Weight control is important to people who have arthritis because extra weight puts extra pressure on some joints and can aggravate many types of arthritis. Diet is especially important for people who have gout. People with gout should avoid alcohol and foods that are high in purines, such as organ meats (liver, kidney), sardines, anchovies, and gravy (NIH Publication No. 02-4999). Does diet therapy relieve your arthritis symptoms? If you don't know, you should talk to your doctor before using diet therapy.

62

Exercise Therapy

BENEFIT FROM EXERCISE THERAPY. People with a rheumatic disease such as arthritis can participate in a variety of sports and exercise programs. Physical exercise can reduce joint pain and stiffness and increase flexibility, muscle strength, and endurance. It also helps with weight reduction and contributes to an improved sense of well-being (NIH Publication No. 02-4999). Does exercise therapy relieve your arthritis symptoms? If you don't know, you should talk to your doctor before using exercise therapy.

63

Friends and Family

BENEFIT FROM FRIENDS AND FAMILY. Friends and family members can help a patient with a rheumatic condition by learning about that condition and understanding how it affects the patient's life. Friends and family can provide emotional and physical assistance. Their support, as well as support from other people who have the same disease, can make it easier to cope. The Arthritis Foundation has a wealth of information to help people with arthritis (NIH Publication No. 02-4999).

64

Heat Therapy

BENEFIT FROM HEAT THERAPY. Heat therapy increases blood flow, tolerance for pain, and flexibility. Heat therapy can involve treatment with paraffin wax, microwaves, ultrasound, or moist heat. Physical therapists are needed for some of these therapies, such as microwave or ultrasound therapy, but patients can apply moist heat include placing warm towels or hot packs on the inflamed joint or taking a warm bath or shower (NIH Publication No. 02-4999). Does heat therapy relieve your arthritis symptoms? If you don't know, you should talk to your doctor before using heat therapy.

65

Home

BENEFIT FROM CHANGES IN THE HOME. Changes in the home may help a person with chronic arthritis continue to live safely, productively, and with less pain. People with arthritis may become weak, lose their balance, or fall. In the bathroom, installing grab bars in the tub or shower and by the toilet, placing a secure seat in the tub, and raising the height of the toilet seat can help. Special kitchen utensils can accommodate hands affected by arthritis to make meal preparation easier. An occupational therapist can help people who have rheumatic conditions identify and make adjustments in their homes to create a safer, more comfortable, and more efficient environment (NIH Publication No. 02-4999).

66

Hydrotherapy

BENEFIT FROM HYDROTHERAPY. Hydrotherapy involves exercising or relaxing in warm water. The water takes some weight off painful joints, making it easier to exercise. It helps relax tense muscles and relieve pain (NIH Publication No. 02-4999). Does hydrotherapy relieve your arthritis symptoms? If you don't know, you should talk to your doctor before using hydrotherapy.

67

Journal

BENEFIT FROM USING A JOURNAL. It may be helpful for people to keep a daily journal that describes the pain. Patients should write down what the affected joint looks like, how it feels, how long the pain lasts, and what they were doing when the pain started (NIH Publication No. 02-4999).

68

Medical History

BENEFIT FROM YOUR MEDICAL HISTORY. It is vital for people with joint pain to give the doctor a complete medical history. Answers to the following questions will help the doctor make an accurate diagnosis.

- Is the pain in one or more joints?
- When does the pain occur?
- How long does the pain last?
- When did you first notice the pain?
- What were you doing when you first noticed the pain?
- Does activity make the pain better or worst?
- Have you had any illnesses or accidents that may account for the pain?
- Is there a family history of any arthritis or other rheumatic disease?
- What medicine(s) are you taking?

Because rheumatic diseases are so diverse and sometimes involve several parts of the body, the doctor may ask many other questions (NIH Publication No. 02-4999).

69

Medications

BENEFIT FROM USING MEDICATIONS. Medications commonly used to treat rheumatic diseases provide relief from pain and inflammation. In some cases, the medication may slow the course of the disease and prevent further damage to joints or other parts of the body.

The doctor may delay using medications until a definite diagnosis is made because medications can hide important symptoms (such as fever and swelling) and thereby interfere with diagnosis. Patients taking any medication, either prescription or over-the-counter, should always follow the doctor's instructions. The doctor should be notified immediately if the medicine is making the symptoms worse or causing other problems, such as upset stomach, nausea, or headache. They may be able to change the dosage or medicine to reduce these side effects (NIH Publication No. 02-4999). Do medications relieve your arthritis symptoms? If you don't know, you should talk to your doctor before using medications.

70

Mobilization Therapy

BENEFIT FROM USING MOBILIZATION THERAPY. Mobilization therapies include traction (gentle, steady pulling), massage, and manipulation. (Someone other than the patient moves stiff joints through their normal range of motion.) When done by a trained professional, these methods can help control pain, increase joint motion, and improve muscle and tendon flexibility (NIH Publication No. 02-4999). Does mobilization therapy relieve your arthritis symptoms? If you don't know, you should talk to your doctor before using mobilization therapy.

71

Nutritional Supplements

BENEFIT FROM USING NUTRITIONAL SUPPLEMENTS. Nutritional supplements are often reported as helpful in treating rheumatic diseases. These include products such as S-adenosylmethionine (SAM-e) for osteoarthritis and fibromyalgia, dehydroepiandrosterone (DHEA) for lupus, and glucosamine and chondroitin sulfate for osteoarthritis. Reports on the safety and effectiveness of these products should be viewed with caution since very few claims have been carefully evaluated (NIH Publication No. 02-4999). Do nutritional supplements relieve your arthritis symptoms? If you don't know, you should talk to your doctor before using nutritional supplements.

72

Physical Examination and Laboratory Tests

BENEFIT FROM PHYSICAL EXAMINATION AND LABORATORY TESTS. The doctor will examine the patient's joints for redness, warmth, damage, ease of movement, and tenderness. Because some forms of arthritis, such as lupus, may affect other organs, a complete physical examination that includes the heart, lungs, abdomen, nervous system, eyes, ears, and throat may be necessary. The doctor may order some laboratory tests to help confirm a diagnosis. Samples of blood, urine, or synovial fluid (lubricating fluid found in the joint) may be needed for the tests (NIH Publication No. 02-4999).

73

Relaxation Therapy

BENEFIT FROM USING RELAXATION THERAPY. Relaxation therapy helps reduce pain by teaching people various ways to release muscle tension throughout the body. In one method of relaxation therapy, known as progressive relaxation, the patient tightens a muscle group and then slowly releases the tension. Doctors and physical therapists can teach patients a variety of relaxation techniques (NIH Publication No. 02-4999). Does relaxation therapy relieve your arthritis symptoms? If you don't know, you should talk to your doctor before using relaxation therapy.

74

Rest Therapy

BENEFIT FROM USING REST THERAPY. People who have a rheumatic disease should develop a comfortable balance between rest and activity. One sign of many rheumatic conditions is fatigue. Patients must pay attention to signals from their bodies. For example, when experiencing pain or fatigue, it is important to take a break and rest. Too much rest, however, may cause muscles and joints to become stiff (NIH Publication No. 02-4999). Does rest relieve your arthritis symptoms? If you don't know, you should talk to your doctor before using rest therapy.

75

Treatments

BENEFIT FROM TREATMENTS. Treatments for rheumatic diseases include rest and relaxation, exercise, proper diet, medication, and instruction about the proper use of joints and ways to conserve energy. Other treatments include the use of pain relief methods and assistive devices, such as splints or braces. In severe cases, surgery may be necessary. The doctor and the patient work together to develop a treatment plan that helps the patient maintain or improve his or her lifestyle. Treatment plans usually combine several types of treatment and vary depending on the rheumatic condition and the patient (NIH Publication No. 02-4999).

76

Unscented Products

BENEFIT FROM UNSCENTED PRODUCTS. Unscented products or fragrance-free (i.e. aftershave lotion, body lotions, cosmetics; deodorants, detergents, fabric softeners, shampoos, liquid soaps, etc.) can provide relief to people with arthritis who suffer from inflammation and swelling of the joints. It is better to use unscented liquid soap, dermatologist tested, dye-free, hypoallergenic, when bathing or washing your hands. You may also want to use rubber gloves when washing dishes.

77

X Rays and
Other Imaging Procedures

BENEFIT FROM X RAYS AND OTHER IMAGING PROCEDURES. To see what the joint looks like inside, the doctor may order x rays or other imaging procedures. X rays provide an image of the bones, but they do not show cartilage, muscles, and ligaments. Other noninvasive imaging methods such as computed tomography (CT or CAT scan), magnetic resonance imaging (MRI), and arthrography show the whole joint. The doctor may look for damage to a joint by using an arthroscope, and small, flexible tube which is inserted through a small incision at the joint and which transmits the image of the inside of a joint to a video screen (NIH Publication No. 02-4999).

78

Your Doctor

BENEFIT FROM YOUR DOCTOR. The role you play in planning your treatment is very important. It is vital for you to have a good relationship with your doctor in order to work together. You should not be afraid to ask questions about your condition or treatment. You must understand the treatment plan and tell the doctor whether or not it is helping you. Research has shown that patients who are well informed and participate actively in their own care experience less pain and make fewer visits to the doctor (NIH Publication No. 02-4999).

PART THREE

Healing Resulting from Faith

When he was come down from the mountain, great multitudes followed him. And, behold, there came a leper and worshipped him, saying, Lord, if thou wilt, thou canst make me clean. And Jesus put forth his hand and touched him, saying, I will; be thou clean. And immediately his leprosy was cleansed. And Jesus said unto him, See thou tell no man; but go thy way, shew thyself to the priest, and offer the gift that Moses commanded, for a testimony unto them. And when Jesus was entered into Capernaum, there came unto him a centurion, beseeching him, And saying, Lord, my servant lieth at home sick of the palsy, grievously tormented. And Jesus saith unto him, I will come and heal him. The centurion answered and said, Lord, I am not worthy that thou shouldest come under my roof: but speak the word only, and my servant shall be healed. For I am a man under authority, having soldiers under me: and I say to this man, Go, and he goeth; and to another, Come, and he cometh; and to my servant, Do this, and he doeth it. (Matthew 8:1-9).

79

Jesus Heals a Centurion's Servant

When Jesus heard it, he marveled, and said to them that followed, Verily I say unto you, I have not found so great faith, no, not in Israel. And I say unto you, That many shall come from the east and west, and shall sit down with Abraham, and Isaac, and Jacob, in the kingdom of heaven. But the children of the kingdom shall be cast out into outer darkness: there shall be weeping and gnashing of teeth. And Jesus said unto the centurion, Go thy way; and as thou hast believed, so be it done unto thee. And his servant was healed in the selfsame hour. (Matthew 8:10-13).

PART FOUR

Healing Resulting from God's Word

He sent his word, and healed them, and delivered them from their destructions. Oh that men would praise the LORD for his goodness, and for his wonderful works to the children of men! (Psalms 107:20-21).

80

Agreeableness

BENEFIT FROM AGREEABLENESS. Verily I say unto you, Whatsoever ye shall bind on earth shall be bound in heaven: and whatsoever ye shall loose on earth shall be loosed in heaven. Again I say unto you, that if two of you shall agree on earth as touching any thing that they shall ask, it shall be done for them of my Father which is in heaven. For where two or three are gathered together in my name, there am I in the midst of them. (Matthew 18:18-20).

81

Ambition

BENEFIT FROM AMBITION. I press toward the mark for the prize of the high calling of God in Christ Jesus. Let us therefore, as many as be perfect, be thus minded: and if in any thing ye be otherwise minded, God shall reveal even this unto you. (Philippians 3:14-15).

82

Charity

BENEFIT FROM CHARITY. And above all things have fervent charity among yourselves: for charity shall cover the multitude of sins. Use hospitality one to another without grudging. As every man hath received the gift, even so minister the same one to another, as good stewards of the manifold grace of God. (1 Peter 4:8-10).

83

Cheerfulness

BENEFIT FROM CHEERFULNESS. But this I say, He which soweth sparingly shall reap also sparingly; and he which soweth bountifully shall reap also bountifully. Every man according as he purposeth in his heart, so let him give; not grudgingly, or of necessity: for God loveth a cheerful giver. (2 Corinthians 9:6-7).

84

Compassion

BENEFIT FROM COMPASSION. And of some have compassion, making a difference; And others save with fear, pulling them out of the fire; hating even the garment spotted by the flesh. Now unto him that is able to keep you from falling, and to present you faultless before the presence of his glory with exceeding joy, To the only wise God our Saviour, be glory and majesty, dominion and power, both now and for ever. Amen. (Jude 1:22-25).

85

Confession

BENEFIT FROM CONFESSION. But what saith it? The word is nigh thee, even in thy mouth, and in thy heart: that is, the word of faith, which we preach; That if thou shalt confess with thy mouth the Lord Jesus, and shalt believe in thine heart that God hath raised him from the dead, thou shalt be saved. For with the heart man believeth unto righteousness; and with the mouth confession is made unto salvation. For the scripture saith, whosoever believeth on him shall not be ashamed. (Romans 10:8-11).

86

Confidence

BENEFIT FROM CONFIDENCE. Cast not away therefore your confidence, which hath great recompense of reward. For ye have need of patience, that, after ye have done the will of God, ye might receive the promise. For yet a little while, and he that shall come will come, and will not tarry. (Hebrews 10:35-37).

87

Conscience

BENEFIT FROM CONSCIENCE. Having a good conscience; that, whereas they speak evil of you, as of evildoers, they may be ashamed that falsely accuse your good conversation in Christ. For it is better, if the will of God be so, that ye suffer for well doing, than for evil doing. (1 Peter 3:16-17).

88

Contentment

BENEFIT FROM CONTENTMENT. But godliness with contentment is great gain. For we brought nothing into this world, and it is certain we can carry nothing out. And having food and raiment let us be therewith content. (1 Timothy 6:6-8).

89

Courtesy

BENEFIT FROM COURTESY. Finally, be ye all of one mind, having compassion one of another, love as brethren, be pitiful, be courteous: Not rendering evil for evil, or railing for railing: but contrariwise blessing; knowing that ye are there-unto called, that ye should inherit a blessing. (1 Peter 3:8-9).

90

Deeds

BENEFIT FROM DEEDS. Wherefore, if I come, I will remember his deeds which he doeth, prating against us with malicious words: and not content therewith, neither doth he himself receive the brethren, and forbiddeth them that would, casteth them out of the church. Beloved, follow not that which is evil, but that which is good. He that doeth good is of God: but he that doeth evil hath not seen God. (3 John 10-11).

91

Diligence

BENEFIT FROM DILIGENCE. And beside this, giving all diligence, add to your faith virtue; and to virtue knowledge; And to knowledge temperance; and to temperance patience; and to patience godliness; And to godliness brotherly kindness; and to brotherly kindness charity. For if these things be in you, and abound, they make you that ye shall neither be barren nor unfruitful in the knowledge of our Lord Jesus Christ. But he that lacketh these things is blind, and cannot see afar off, and hath forgotten that he was purged from his old sins. Wherefore the rather, brethren, give diligence to make your calling and election sure: for if ye do these things, ye shall never fall: For so an entrance shall be ministered unto you abundantly into the everlasting kingdom of our Lord and Saviour Jesus Christ. (2 Peter 1:5-11).

92

Faith

BENEFIT FROM FAITH. And Jesus answering saith unto them, Have faith in God. For verily I say unto you. That whosoever shall say unto this mountain, Be thou removed, and be thou cast into the sea; and shall not doubt in his heart, but shall believe that those things which he saith shall come to pass; he shall have whatsoever he saith. Therefore I say unto you, What things soever ye desire, when ye pray, believe that ye receive them, and ye shall have them. (Mark 11:22-24).

93

Forgiveness

BENEFIT FROM FOREGIVENESS. For if ye forgive men their trespasses, your heavenly Father will also forgive you: but if ye forgive not men their trespasses, neither will your Father forgive your trespasses. (Mathew 6:14-15).

94

Fruit of the Spirit

BENEFIT FROM FRUIT OF THE SPIRIT. But the fruit of the Spirit is love, joy, peace, longsuffering, gentleness, goodness, faith, Meekness, temperance: against such there is no law. And they that are Christ's have crucified the flesh with the affections and lusts. If we live in the Spirit, let us also walk in the Spirit. Let us not be desirous of vain glory, provoking one another, envying one another. (Galatians 5:22-26).

95

Godliness

BENEFIT FROM GODLINESS. But refuse profane and old wives' fables, and exercise thyself rather unto godliness. For bodily exercise profiteth little: but godliness is profitable unto all things, having promise of the life that now is, and of that which is to come. This is a faithful saying and worthy of all acceptation. (1 Timothy 4:7-9).

96

Gratitude

BENEFIT FROM GRATITUDE. But thanks be to God, which giveth us the victory through our Lord Jesus Christ. Therefore, my beloved brethren, be ye stedfast, unmoveable, always abounding in the work of the Lord, forasmuch as ye know that your labour is not in vain in the Lord. (1 Corinthians 15:57-58).

97

Holy Scripture

BENEFIT FROM HOLY SCRIPTURE. We then that are strong ought to bear the infirmities of the weak, and not to please ourselves. Let every one of us please his neighbour for his good to edification. For even Christ pleased not himself; but, as it is written, The reproaches of them that reproached thee fell on me. For whatsoever things were written aforetime were written for our learning, that we through patience and comfort of the scriptures might have hope. (Romans 15:1-4).

98

Holy Spirit

BENEFIT FROM HOLY SPIRIT. For we are saved by hope: but hope that is seen is not hope: for what a man seeth, why doth he yet hope for? But if we hope for that we see not, then do we with patience wait for it. Likewise the Spirit also helpeth our infirmities: for we know not what we should pray for as we ought: but the Spirit itself maketh intercession for us with groanings which cannot be uttered. And he that searcheth the hearts knoweth what is the mind of the Spirit, because he maketh intercession for the saints according to the will of God. And we know that all things work together for good to them that love God, to them who are the called according to this purpose. (Romans 8:24-28).

99

Hope

BENEFIT FROM HOPE. For as the sufferings of Christ abound in us, so our consolation also aboundeth by Christ. And whether we be afflicted, it is for your consolation and salvation, which is effectual in the enduring of the same sufferings which we also suffer: or whether we be comforted, it is for your consolation and salvation. And our hope of you is stedfast, knowing, that as ye are partakers of the sufferings, so shall ye be also of the consolation. (2 Corinthians 1:5-7).

100

Joy

BENEFIT FROM JOY. Now the parable is this: The seed is the word of God. Those by the way side are they that hear; then cometh the devil, and taketh away the word out of their hearts, lest they should believe and be saved. They on the rock are they, which, when they hear, receive the word with joy; and these have no root, which for a while believe, and in time of temptation fall away. (Luke 8:11-13).

101

Kindness

BENEFIT FROM KINDNESS. Let all bitterness, and wrath, and anger, and clamour, and evil speaking, be put away from you, with all malice: And be ye kind one to another, tenderhearted, forgiving one another, even as God for Christ's sake hath forgiven you. (Ephesians 4:31-32).

102

Kingdom of God

BENEFIT FROM KINGDOM OF GOD. Therefore take no thought, saying, What shall we eat? Or, What shall we drink? Or, Wherewithal shall we be clothed? (For after all these things do the Gentiles seek:) for your heavenly Father knoweth that ye have need of all these things. But seek ye first the kingdom of God, and his righteousness; and all these things shall be added unto you. (Matthew 6:31-33).

103

Knowledge

BENEFIT FROM KNOWLEDGE. All the words of my mouth are in righteousness; there is nothing froward or perverse in them. They are all plain to him that understandeth, and right to them that find knowledge. Receive my instruction, and not silver; and knowledge rather than choice gold. For wisdom is better than rubies; and all the things that may be desired are not to be compared to it. (Proverbs 8:8-11).

104

Love

BENEFIT FROM LOVE. Beloved, let us love one another: for love is of God; and every one that loveth is born of God, and knoweth God. He that loveth not knoweth not God; for God is love. In this was manifested the love of God toward us, because that God sent his only begotten Son into the world, that we might live through him. Herein is love, not that we loved God, but that he loved us, and sent his Son to be the propitiation for our sins. Beloved, if God so loved us, we ought also to love one another. (1 John 4:7-11).

105

Meekness

BENEFIT FROM MEEKNESS. I therefore, the prisoner of the Lord, beseech you that ye walk worthy of the vocation wherewith ye are called, With all lowliness and meekness, with longsuffering, forbearing one another in love; Endeavouring to keep the unity of the Spirit in the bond of peace. (Ephesians 4:1-3).

106

Mercy

BENEFIT FROM MERCY. Put on therefore, as the elect of God, holy and beloved, bowels of mercies, kindness, humbleness of mind, meekness, longsuffering; Forbearing one another, and forgiving one another, if any man have a quarrel against any; even as Christ forgave you, so also do ye. (Colossians 3:12-13).

107

Patience

BENEFIT FROM PATIENCE. And we desire that every one of you do show the same diligence to the full assurance of hope unto the end: That ye be not slothful, but followers of them who through faith and patience inherit the promises. (Hebrews 6:11-12).

108

Peacemaking

BENEFIT FROM PEACEMAKING. Let not then your good be evil spoken of: For the kingdom of God is not meat and drink; but righteousness, and peace, and joy in the Holy Ghost. For he that in these things serveth Christ is acceptable to God, and approved of men. Let us therefore follow after the things which make for peace, and things wherewith one may edify another. (Romans 14:16-19).

109

Prayer

BENEFIT FROM PRAYER. After this manner therefore pray ye: Our Father which art in heaven, Hallowed be thy name. Thy kingdom come. Thy will be done in earth, as it is in heaven. Give us this day our daily bread. And forgive us our debts, as we forgive our debtors. And lead us not into temptation, but deliver us from evil: For thine is the kingdom, and the power, and the glory, for ever, Amen. (Matthew 6:9-13).

110

Pureness

BENEFIT FROM PURENESS. If a man therefore purge himself from these, he shall be a vessel unto honour, sanctified, and meet for the master's use, and prepared unto every good work. Flee also youthful lusts: but follow righteousness, faith, charity, peace, with them that call on the Lord out of a pure heart. (2 Timothy 2:21-22).

111

Regeneration

BENEFIT FROM REGENERATION. Jesus answered and said unto him, Verily, verily, I say unto thee, Except a man be born again, he cannot see the kingdom of God. Nicodemus saith unto him, How can a man be born when he is old? can he enter the second time into his mother's womb, and be born? Jesus answered, Verily, verily, I say unto thee, Except a man be born of water and of the Spirit, he cannot enter into the kingdom of God. That which is born of the flesh is flesh; and that which is born of the Spirit is spirit. Marvel not that I said unto thee, Ye must be born again. The wind bloweth where it listeth, and thou hearest the sound thereof, but canst not tell whence it cometh, and whither it goeth: so is every one that is born of the Spirit. (John 3:3-8).

112

Repentance

BENEFIT FROM REPENTANCE. Now after that John was put in prison, Jesus came into Galilee, preaching the gospel of the kingdom of God. And saying, The time is fulfilled, and the kingdom of God is at hand: repent ye, and believe the gospel. (Mark 1:14-15).

113

Temperance

BENEFIT FROM TEMPERANCE. Know ye not that they which run in a race run all, but one receiveth the prize? So run, that ye may obtain. And every man that striveth for the mastery is temperate in all things. Now they do it to obtain a corruptible crown; but we an incorruptible. I therefore so run, not as uncertainly; so fight I, not as one that beateth the air: But I keep under my body, and bring it into subjection: lest that by any means, when I have preached to others, I myself should be a castaway. (1 Corinthians 9:24-27).

114

Virtue

BENEFIT FROM VIRTUE. Finally, brethren, whatsoever things are true, whatsoever things are honest, whatsoever things are just, whatsoever things are pure, whatsoever things are lovely, whatsoever things are of good report; if there be any virtue, and if there be any praise, think on these things. Those things, which ye have both learned, and received, and heard, and seen in me, do: and the God of peace shall be with you. (Philippians 4:8-9).

PART FIVE

Healing Resulting from Intercession

Likewise the Spirit also helpeth our infirmities: for we know not what we should pray for as we ought: but the Spirit itself maketh intercession for us with groanings which cannot be uttered. And he that searcheth the hearts knoweth what is the mind of the Spirit, because he maketh intercession for the saints according to the will of God. And we know that all things work together for good to them that love God, to them who are the called according to his purpose. For whom he did foreknow, he also did predestinate to be conformed to the image of his Son, that he might be the firstborn among many brethren. (Romans 8:26-29).

115

Christ Intercedes for Us

Moreover whom he did predestinate, them he also called: and whom he called, them he also justified: and whom he justified, them he also glorified. What shall we then say to these things? If God be for us, who can be against us? He that spared not his own Son, but delivered him up for us all, how shall he not with him also freely give us all things? Who shall lay anything to the charge of God's elect? It is God that justifieth. Who is he that condemneth? It is Christ that died, yea rather, that is risen again, who is even at the right hand of God, who also maketh intercession for us. (Romans 8:30-34).

PART SIX

Healing Resulting from Prayer

Is any among you afflicted? Let him pray. Is any merry? Let him sing psalms. Is any sick among you? Let him call for the elders of the church and let them pray over him, anointing him with oil in the name of the Lord: And the prayer of faith shall save the sick, and the Lord shall raise him up; and if he have committed sins, they shall be forgiven him. (James 5:13-15).

116

Elias Prays

Confess your faults one to another, and pray one for another, that ye may be healed. The effectual fervent prayer of a righteous man availeth much. Elias was a man subject to like passions as we are, and he prayed earnestly that it might not rain: and it rained not on the earth by the space of three years and six months. And he prayed again, and the heaven gave rain, and the earth brought forth her fruit. Brethren, if any of you do err from the truth, and one convert him; Let him know, that he which converteth the sinner from the error of his way, shall save a soul from death, and shall hide a multitude of sins. (James 5:16-20).

PART SEVEN

Healing Resulting from Repentance

Remember therefore from whence thou art fallen, and repent, and do the first works; or else I will come unto thee quickly, and will remove thy candlestick out of his place, except thou repent. But this thou hast, that thou hatest the deeds of the Nicolaitans, which I also hate. He that hath an ear, let him hear what the Spirit saith unto the churches; To him that overcometh will I give to eat of the tree of life, which is in the midst of the paradise of God. (Revelation 2:5-7).

117

Adultery

REPENT FROM ADULTERY. They say unto him, Why did Moses then command to give a writing of divorcement, and to put her away? He saith unto them, Moses because of the hardness of your hearts suffered you to put away your wives: but from the beginning it was not so. And I say unto you, Whosoever shall put away his wife, except it be for fornication, and shall marry another, committeth adultery: and whoso marrieth her which is put away doth commit adultery. (Matthew 19:7-9).

118

Anger

REPENT FROM ANGER. A soft answer turneth away wrath: but grievous words stir up anger. The tongue of the wise useth knowledge aright: but the mouth of fools poureth out foolishness. The eyes of the LORD are in every place, beholding the evil and the good. (Proverbs 15:1-3).

119

Boasting

REPENT FROM BOASTING. Boast not thyself of tomorrow; for thou knowest not what a day may bring forth. Let another man praise thee, and not thine own mouth; a stranger, and not thine own lips. (Proverbs 27:1-2).

120

Covetousness

REPENT FROM COVETOUSNESS. Let your conversation be without covetousness; and be content with such things as ye have: for he hath said, I will never leave thee, nor forsake thee. So that we may boldly say, The Lord is my helper, and I will not fear what man shall do unto me. Remember them which have the rule over you, who have spoken unto you the word of God: whose faith follow, considering the end of their conversation. Jesus Christ the same yesterday, and to day, and for ever. (Hebrews 13:5-8).

121

Cowardice

REPENT FROM COWARDICE. The fear of man bringeth a snare: but whoso putteth his trust in the LORD shall be safe. Many seek the ruler's favour; but every man's judgment cometh from the LORD. An unjust man is an abomination to the just: and he that is upright in the way is abomination to the wicked. (Proverbs 29:25-27).

122

Deceitfulness

.

REPENT FROM DECEITFULNESS. Thine habitation is in the midst of deceit; through deceit they refuse to know me, saith the LORD. Therefore thus saith the LORD of hosts, Behold, I will melt them, and try them, for how shall I do for the daughter of my people? Their tongue is as an arrow shot out; it speaketh deceit: one speaketh peaceably to his neighbour with his mouth, but in heart he layeth his wait. (Jeremiah 9:6-8).

123

Despair

REPENT FROM DESPAIR. Humble yourselves therefore under the mighty hand of God, that he may exalt you in due time: Casting all your care upon him: for he careth for you. Be sober, be vigilant; because your adversary the devil, as a roaring lion, walketh about, seeking whom he may devour: Whom resist stedfast in the faith, knowing that the same afflictions are accomplished in your brethren that are in the world. But the God of all grace, who hath called us unto his eternal glory by Christ Jesus, after that ye have suffered a while, make you perfect, stablish, strengthen, settle you. To him be glory and dominion for ever and ever. Amen. (1 Peter 5:6-11).

124

Despondency

REPENT FROM DESPONDENCY. Hast thou not known? Hast thou not heard, that the everlasting God, the LORD, the Creator of the ends of the earth, fainteth not, neither is weary? There is no searching of his understanding. He giveth power to the faint; and to them that have no might he increaseth strength. Even the youths shall faint and be weary, and the young men shall utterly fall: But they that wait upon the LORD shall renew their strength; they shall mount up with wings as eagles; they shall run, and not be weary; and they shall walk, and not faint. (Isaiah 40:28-31).

125

Discouragement

REPENT FROM DISCOURAGEMENT. He hath delivered my soul in peace from the battle that was against me: for there were many with me. God shall hear, and afflict them, even he that abideth of old. Selah. Because they have no changes, therefore they fear not God. He hath put forth his hands against such as be at peace with him: he hath broken his covenant. The words of his mouth were smoother than butter, but war was in his heart: his words were softer than oil, yet were they drawn swords. Cast thy burden upon the LORD, and he shall sustain thee: he shall never suffer the righteous to be moved. But thou, O God, shalt bring them down into the pit of destruction: bloody and deceitful men shall not live out half their days: but I will trust in thee. (Psalm 55:18-23).

126

Discourtesy

REPENT FROM RUDENESS. Let brotherly love continue. Be not forgetful to entertain strangers: for thereby some have entertained angels unawares. (Hebrews 13:1-2).

127

Dishonesty

REPENT FROM DISHONESTY. When the morning was come, all the chief priests and elders of the people took counsel against Jesus to put him to death: And when they had bound him, they led him away, and delivered him to Pontius Pilate the governor. Then Judas, which had betrayed him, when he saw that he was condemned, repented himself, and brought again the thirty pieces of silver to the chief priests and elders, Saying, I have sinned in that I have betrayed the innocent blood. And they said, What is that to us? See thou to that. And he cast down the pieces of silver in the temple, and departed, and went and hanged himself. (Matthew 27:1-5).

128

Disobedience

REPENT FROM DISOBEDIENCE. For as by one man's disobedience many were made sinners, so by the obedience of one shall many be made righteous. Moreover the law entered, that the offence might abound. But where sin abounded, grace did much more abound: That as sin hath reigned unto death, even so might grace reign through righteousness unto eternal life by Jesus Christ our Lord. (Romans 5:19-21).

129

Divorce

REPENT FROM DIVORCE. And unto the married I command, yet not I, but the Lord, let not the wife depart from her husband: But and if she depart, let her remain unmarried, or be reconciled to her husband: and let not the husband put away his wife. But to the rest speak I, not the Lord: If any brother hath a wife that believeth not, and she be pleased to dwell with him, let him not put her away. And the woman which hath an husband that believeth not, and if he be pleased to dwell with her, let her not leave him. For the unbelieving husband is sanctified by the wife, and the unbelieving wife is sanctified by the husband: else were your children unclean; but now are they holy. But if the unbelieving depart, let him depart. A brother or a sister is not under bondage in such cases: but God hath called us to peace. (1 Corinthians 7:10-15).

130

Double-mindedness

REPENT FROM DOUBLE-MINDEDNESS. A double minded man is unstable in all his ways. Let the brother of low degree rejoice in that he is exalted: But the rich, in that he is made low: because as the flower of the grass he shall pass away. For the sun is no sooner risen with a burning heat, but it withereth the grass, and the flower thereof falleth, and the grace of the fashion of it perisheth: so also shall the rich man fade away in his ways. (James 1:8-11).

131

Drunkenness

REPENT FROM DRUNKENNESS. But if ye be led of the Spirit, ye are not under the law. Now the works of the flesh are manifest, which are these; Adultery, fornication, uncleanness, lasciviousness, Idolatry, witchcraft, hatred, variance, emulations, wrath, strife, seditions, heresies, Envyings, murders, drunkenness, revellings, and such like: of the which I tell you before, as I have also told you in time past, that they which do such things shall not inherit the kingdom of God. (Galatians 5:18-21).

132

Evil Deeds

REPENT FROM EVIL DEEDS. For many deceivers are entered into the world, who confess not that Jesus Christ is come in the flesh. This is a deceiver and an antichrist. Look to yourselves, that we lose not those things which we have wrought, but that we receive a full reward. Whosoever transgresseth, and abideth not in the doctrine of Christ, hath not God. He that abideth in the doctrine of Christ, he hath both the Father and the Son. If there come any unto you, and bring not this doctrine, receive him not into your house, neither bid him God speed: For he that biddeth him God speed is partaker of his evil deeds. (2 John 7-11).

133

Excuses

REPENT FROM EXCUSES. And when one of them that sat at meat with him heard these things, he said unto him, Blessed is he that shall eat bread in the kingdom of God. Then said he unto him, A certain man made a great supper, and bade many: And sent his servant at supper time to say to them that were bidden, Come: for all things are now ready. And they all with one consent began to make excuse. The first said unto him, I have bought a piece of ground, and I must needs go and see it: I pray thee have me excused. And another said, I have bought five yoke of oxen, and I go to prove them: I pray thee have me excused. And another said, I have married a wife, and therefore I cannot come. So that servant came, and showed his lord these things. Then the master of the house being angry said to his servant, Go out quickly into the streets and lanes of the city, and bring in hither the poor, and the maimed, and the halt, and the blind. And the servant said, Lord, it is done as thou hast commanded, and yet there is room. And the lord said unto the servant, Go out into the highways and hedges, and compel them to come in, that my house may be filled. For I say unto you, That none of those men which were bidden shall taste of my supper. (Luke 14:15-24).

134

Faultfinding

REPENT FROM FAULTFINDING. And it came to pass, that, as Jesus sat at meat in his house, many publicans and sinners sat also together with Jesus and his disciples: for there were many, and they followed him. And when the scribes and Pharisees saw him eat with publicans and sinners, they said unto his disciples, How is it that he eateth and drinketh with publicans and sinners? When Jesus heard it, he saith unto them, They that are whole have no need of the physician, but they that are sick: I came not to call the righteous, but sinners to repentance. (Mark 2:15-17).

135

Fear

REPENT FROM FEAR. The LORD is my light and my salvation; whom shall I fear? The LORD is the strength of my life; of whom shall I be afraid? When the wicked, even mine enemies and my foes, came upon me to eat up my flesh, they stumbled and fell. Though an host should encamp against me, my heart shall not fear: though war should rise against me, in this will I be confident. One thing have I desired of the LORD, that will I seek after; that I may dwell in the house of the LORD all the days of my life, to behold the beauty of the LORD, and to inquire in his temple. (Psalm 27:1-4).

136

Fickleness

REPENT FROM FICKLENESS. Fret not thyself because of evil men, neither be thou envious at the wicked; For there shall be no reward to the evil man; the candle of the wicked shall be put out. My son, fear thou the LORD and the king: and meddle not with them that are given to change: For their calamity shall rise suddenly; and who knoweth the ruin of them both? These things also belong to the wise. It is not good to have respect of persons in judgment. He that saith unto the wicked, Thou art righteous; him shall the people curse, nations shall abhor him: But to them that rebuke him shall be delight, and a good blessing shall come upon them. (Proverbs 24:19-25).

137

Fornication

REPENT FROM FORNICATION. Now concerning the things whereof ye wrote unto me: It is good for a man not to touch a woman. Nevertheless, to avoid fornication, let every man have his own wife, and let every woman have her own husband. Let the husband render unto the wife due benevolence: and likewise also the wife unto the husband. The wife hath not power of her own body, but the husband: and likewise also the husband hath not power of his own body, but the wife. Defraud ye not one the other, except it be with consent for a time, that ye may give yourselves to fasting and prayer; and come together again, that Satan tempt you not for your incontinency. But I speak this by permission, and not of commandment. For I would that all men were even as I myself. But every man hath his proper gift of God, one after this manner, and another after that. (1 Corinthians 7:1-7).

138

Glutony

REPENT FROM OVER-EATING. Let not thine heart envy sinners: but be thou in the fear of the LORD all the day long. For surely there is an end; and thine expectation shall not be cut off. Hear thou, my son, and be wise, and guide thine heart in the way. Be not among winebibbers; among riotous eaters of flesh: For the drunkard and the glutton shall come to poverty: and drowsiness shall clothe a man with rags. (Proverbs 23:17-21).

139

Greed

REPENT FROM GREED. For we brought nothing into this world, and it is certain we can carry nothing out. And having food and raiment let us be therewith content. But they that will be rich fall into temptation and a snare, and into many foolish and hurtful lusts, which drown men in destruction and perdition. For the love of money is the root of all evil: which while some coveted after, they have erred from the faith, and pierced themselves through with many sorrows. But thou, O man of God, flee these things; and follow after righteousness, godliness, faith, love, patience, meekness. Fight the good fight of faith, lay hold on eternal life, whereunto thou art also called, and has professed a good profession before many witnesses. (1 Timothy 6:7-12).

140

Guilt

REPENT FROM GUILT. But what saith it? The word is nigh thee, even in thy mouth, and in thy heart: that is, the word of faith which we preach; That if thou shalt confess with thy mouth the Lord Jesus, and shall believe in thine heart that God hath raised him from the dead, thou shalt be saved. For with the heart man believeth unto righteousness; and with the mouth confession is made unto salvation. For the scripture saith, Whosoever believeth on him shall not be ashamed. For there is no difference between the Jew and the Greek: for the same Lord over all is rich unto all that call upon him. For whosoever shall call upon the name of the Lord shall be saved. (Romans 10:8-13).

141

Hate

REPENT FROM HATE. Hear instruction, and be wise, and refuse it not. Blessed is the man that heareth me, watching daily at my gates, waiting at the posts of my doors. For whoso findeth me findeth life, and shall obtain favour of the LORD. But he that sinneth against me wrongeth his own soul: all they that hate me love death. (Proverbs 8:33-36).

142

Haughtiness

REPENT FROM ARROGANCE. I wisdom dwell with prudence, and find out knowledge of witty inventions. The fear of the LORD is to hate evil: pride, and arrogancy, and the evil way, and the froward mouth, do I hate. Counsel is mine, and sound wisdom: I am understanding; I have strength. By me kings reign, and princes decree justice. By me princes rule, and nobles, even all the judges of the earth. I love them that love me; and those that seek me early shall find me. Riches and honour are with me; yea, durable riches and righteousness. (Proverbs 8:12-18).

143

Hopelessness

REPENT FROM HOPELESSNESS. For by grace are ye saved through faith; and that not of yourselves: it is the gift of God: Not of works, lest any man should boast. For we are his workmanship, created in Christ Jesus unto good works, which God hath before ordained that we should walk in them. Wherefore remember, that ye being in time past Gentiles in the flesh, who are called Uncircumcision by that which is called the Circumcision in the flesh made by hands; That at that time ye were without Christ, being aliens from the commonwealth of Israel, and strangers from the covenants of promise, having no hope, and without God in the world: But now in Christ Jesus ye who sometimes were far off are made nigh by the blood of Christ. (Ephesians 2:8-13).

144

Idolatry

REPENT FROM IDOLATRY. Wherefore, my dearly beloved, flee from idolatry. I speak as to wise men; judge ye what I say. The cup of blessing which we bless, is it not the communion of the blood of Christ? The bread which we break, is it not the communion of the body of Christ? For we being many are one bread, and one body: for we are all partakers of that one bread. Behold Israel after the flesh: are not they which eat of the sacrifices partakers of the altar? What say I then? That the idol is any thing, or that which is offered in sacrifice to idols is any thing? But I say, that the things which the Gentiles sacrifice, they sacrifice to devils, and not to God: and I would not that ye should have fellowship with devils. Ye cannot drink the cup of the Lord, and the cup of devils: ye cannot be partakers of the Lord's table, and of the table of devils. (1 Corinthians 10:14-21).

145

Immorality

REPENT FROM IMMORALITY. It is reported commonly that there is fornication among you, and such fornication as is not so much as named among the Gentiles, that one should have his father's wife. And ye are puffed up, and have not rather mourned, that he that hath done this deed might be taken away from among you. For I verily, as absent in body, but present in spirit, have judged already, as though I were present, concerning him that hath so done this deed, In the name of our Lord Jesus Christ, when ye are gathered together, and my spirit, with the power of our Lord Jesus Christ, To deliver such an one unto Satan for the destruction of the flesh, that the spirit may be saved in the day of the Lord Jesus. (1 Corinthians 5:1-5).

146

Impatience

REPENT FROM IMPATIENCE. Now the God of patience and consolation grant you to be likeminded one toward another according to Christ Jesus: That ye may with one mind and one mouth glorify God, even the Father of our Lord Jesus Christ. Wherefore receive ye one another, as Christ also received us to the glory of God. (Romans 15:5-7).

147

Indecision

REPENT FROM INDECISION. And he said unto another, Follow me. But he said, Lord, suffer me first to go and bury my father. Jesus said unto him, Let the dead bury their dead: but go thou and preach the kingdom of God. And another also said, Lord, I will follow thee; but let me first go bid them farewell, which are at home at my house. And Jesus said unto him, No man, having put his hand to the plow and looking back, is fit for the kingdom of God. (Luke 9:59-62).

148

Ingratitude

REPENT FROM INGRATITUDE. For the invisible things of him from the creation of the world are clearly seen, being understood by the things that are made, even his eternal power and Godhead; so that they are without excuse: Because that, when they knew God, they glorified him not as God, neither were thankful; but became vain in their imaginations, and their foolish heart was darkened. (Romans 1:20-21).

149

Injustice

REPENT FROM INJUSTICE. My face is foul with weeping, and on my eyelids is the shadow of death; Not for any injustice in mine hands: also my prayer is pure. O earth, cover not thou my blood, and let my cry have no place. Also now, behold, my witness is in heaven, and my record is on high. My friends scorn me: but mine eye poureth out tears unto God. O that one might plead for a man with God, as a man pleadeth for his neighbor! When a few years are come, then I shall go the way whence I shall not return. (Job 16:16-22).

150

Intemperance

REPENT FROM INTEMPERANCE. Apply thine heart unto instruction, and thine ears to the words of knowledge. Withhold not correction from the child: for if thou beatest him with the rod, he shall not die. Thou shalt beat him with the rod, and shalt deliver his soul from hell. My son, if thine heart be wise, my heart shall rejoice, even mine. Yea, my reins shall rejoice, when thy lips speak right things. Let not thine heart envy sinners: but be thou in the fear of the LORD all the day long. For surely there is an end; and thine expectation shall not be cut off. Hear thou, my son, and be wise, and guide thine heart in the way. (Proverbs 23:12-19).

151

Laziness

REPENT FROM LAZINESS. For even when we were with you, this we commanded you, that if any would not work, neither should he eat. For we hear that there are some which walk among you disorderly, working not at all, but are busybodies. Now them that are such we command and exhort by our Lord Jesus Christ, that with quietness they work, and eat their own bread. (2 Thessalonians 3:10-12).

152

Lusts

REPENT FROM LUSTS. But ye are a chosen generation, a royal priesthood, an holy nation, a peculiar people; that ye should show forth the praises of him who hath called you out of darkness into his marvellous light: Which in time past were not a people of God: which had not obtained mercy, but now have obtained mercy. Dearly beloved, I beseech you as strangers and pilgrims, abstain from fleshly lusts, which war against the soul; Having your conversation honest among the Gentiles: that, whereas they speak against you as evildoers, they may be your good works, which they shall behold, glorify God in the day of visitation. (1 Peter 2:9-12).

153

Lying

REPENT FROM LYING. Who is a liar but he that denieth that Jesus is the Christ? He is anticrist, that denieth the Father and the Son. Whosoever denieth the Son, the same hath not the Father: [but] he that acknowledgeth the Son hath the Father also. Let that therefore abide in you, which ye have heard from the beginning. If that which ye have heard from the beginning shall remain in you, ye also shall continue in the Son, and in the Father. And this is the promise that he hath promised us, even eternal life. (1 John 2:22-25).

154

Malice

REPENT FROM MALICE. Wherefore laying aside all malice, and all guile, and hypocrisies, and envies, and all evil speakings, As newborn babes, desire the sincere milk of the word, that ye may grow thereby: If so be ye have tasted that the Lord is gracious. To whom coming, as unto a living stone, disallowed indeed of men, but chosen of God, and precious, Ye also, as lively stones, are built up a spiritual house, an holy priesthood, to offer up spiritual sacrifices, acceptable to God by Jesus Christ. (1 Peter 2:1-5).

155

Parsimony

REPENT FROM STINGINESS. The desire of the righteous is only good: but the expectation of the wicked is wrath. There is that scattereth, and yet increaseth; and there is that withholdeth more than is meet, but it tendeth to poverty. The liberal soul shall be made fat: and he that watereth shall be watered also himself. He that withholdeth corn, the people shall curse him: but blessing shall be upon the head of him that selleth it. He that diligently seeketh good procureth favour: but he that seeketh mischief, it shall come unto him. (Proverbs 11:23-27).

156

Pride

REPENT FROM PRIDE. Why standest thou afar off, O LORD? Why hidest thou thyself in time of trouble? The wicked in his pride doth persecute the poor: let them be taken in the devices that they have imagined. For the wicked boasteth of his heart's desire, and blesseth the covetous, whom the LORD abhorreth. The wicked, through the pride of his countenance, will not seek after God: God is not in all his thoughts. (Psalm 10:1-4).

157

Selfishness

REPENT FROM SELFISHNESS. Do we provoke the Lord to jealously? Are we stronger than he? All things are lawful for me, but all things are not expedient: all things are lawful for me, but all things edify not. Let no man seek his own, but every man another's wealth. Whatsoever is sold in the shambles, that eat, asking no question for conscience sake: For the earth is the Lord's, and the fulness thereof. (1 Corinthians 10:22-26).

158

Sorrow

REPENT FROM SORROW. But I would not have you to be ignorant, brethren, concerning them which are asleep, that ye sorrow not, even as others which have not hope. For if we believe that Jesus died and rose again, even so them also which sleep in Jesus will God bring with him. For this we say unto you by the word of the Lord, that we which are alive and remain unto the coming of the Lord shall not prevent them which are asleep. For the Lord himself shall descend from heaven with a shout, with the voice of the archangel, and with the trump of God: and the dead in Christ shall rise first: Then we which are alive and remain shall be caught up together with them in the clouds, to meet the Lord in the air: and so shall we ever be with the Lord. Wherefore comfort one another with these words. (1 Thessalonians 4:13-18).

159

Strife

REPENT FROM STRIFE. He that passeth by, and meddleth with strife belonging not to him, is like one that taketh a dog by the ears. As a mad man who casteth firebrands, arrows, and death, So is the man that deceiveth his neighbour, and saith, Am not I in sport? Where no wood is, there the fire goeth out: so where there is no talebearer, the strife ceaseth. As coals are to burning coals, and wood to fire; so is a contentious man to kindle strife. (Proverbs 26:17-21).

160

Temptation

REPENT FROM TEMPTATION. Blessed is the man that endureth temptation: for when he is tried, he shall receive the crown of life, which the Lord hath promised to them that love him. Let no man say when he is tempted, I am tempted of God: for God cannot be tempted with evil, neither tempteth he any man: But every man is tempted, when he is drawn away of his own lust, and enticed. Then when lust hath conceived, it bringeth forth sin: and sin, when it is finished, bringeth forth death. (James 1:12-15).

161

Thoughts

REPENT FROM EVIL THOUGHTS. My brethren, have not the faith of our Lord Jesus Christ, the Lord of glory, with respect of persons. For if there come into your assembly a man with a gold ring, in goodly apparel, and there come in also a poor man in vile raiment; And ye have respect to him that weareth the gay clothing, and say unto him, Sit thou here in a good place; and say to the poor, Stand thou there, or sit here under my footstool: Are ye not then partial in yourselves, and are become judges of evil thoughts? (James 2:1-4).

162

Uncleanness

REPENT FROM UNCLEANNESS. For our exhortation was not of deceit, nor of uncleanness, nor in guile: But as we were allowed of God to be put in trust with the gospel, even so we speak; not as pleasing men, but God, which trieth our hearts. For neither at any time used we flattering words, as ye know, nor a cloak of covetousness; God is witness: Nor of men sought we glory, neither of you, nor yet of others, when we might have been burdensome, as the apostles of Christ. (1 Thessalonians 2:3-6).

163

Unfaithfulness

REPENT FROM UNFAITHFULNESS. As the cold of snow in the time of harvest, so is a faithful messenger to them that send him: for he refresheth the soul of his masters. Whoso boasteth himself of a false gift is like clouds and wind without rain. By long forbearing is a prince persuaded, and a soft tongue breaketh the bone. Has thou found honey? Eat so much as is sufficient for thee, lest thou be filled therewith, and vomit it. Withdraw thy foot from thy neighbour's house; lest he be weary of thee, and so hate thee. A man that beareth false witness against his neighbour is a maul, and a sword, and a sharp arrow. Confidence in an unfaithful man in time of trouble is like a broken tooth, and a foot out of joint. (Proverbs 25:13-19).

164

Unfruitfulness

REPENT FROM UNFRUITFULNESS. Bring Zenas the lawyer and
Apollos on their journey diligently, that nothing be wanting unto them. And
let ours also learn to maintain good works for necessary uses, that they be
not unfruitful. All that are with me salute thee. Greet them that love us in
the faith. Grace be with you all. Amen. (Titus 3:13-15).

165

Ungodliness

REPENT FROM UNGODLINESS. For I am not ashamed of the gospel of Christ: for it is the power of God unto salvation to every one that believeth; to the Jew first, and also to the Greek. For therein is the righteousness of God revealed from faith to faith: as it is written, The just shall live by faith. For the wrath of God is revealed from heaven against all ungodliness and unrighteousness of men, who hold the truth in unrighteousness: Because that which may be known of God is manifest in them; for God hath showed it unto them. (Romans 1:16-19).

166

Unmercifulness

REPENT FROM UNMERCIFULNESS. But, beloved, remember ye the words which were spoken before of the apostles of our Lord Jesus Christ; How that they told you there should be mockers in the last time, who should walk after their own ungodly lusts. These be they who separate themselves, sensual, having not the Spirit. But ye, beloved, building up yourselves on your most holy faith, praying in the Holy Ghost, Keep yourselves in the love of God, looking for the mercy of our Lord Jesus Christ unto eternal life. (Jude 1:17-21).

167

Unrighteousness

REPENT FROM UNRIGHTEOUSNESS. Know ye not that the unrighteous shall not inherit the kingdom of God? Be not deceived: neither fornicators, nor idolaters, nor adulterers, nor effeminate, nor abusers of themselves with mankind. Nor thieves, nor covetous, nor drunkards, nor revilers, nor extortioners, shall inherit the kingdom of God. And such were some of you: but ye are washed, but ye are sanctified, but ye are justified in the name of the Lord Jesus, and by the Spirit of our God. (1 Corinthians 6:9-11).

168

Unthankfulness

REPENT FROM UNTHANKFULNESS. This know also, that in the last days perilous times shall come. For men shall be lovers of their own selves, covetous, boasters, proud, blasphemers, disobedient to parents, unthankful, unholy, Without natural affection, trucebreakers, false accusers, incontinent, fierce, despisers of those that are good, Traitors, heady, highminded, lovers of pleasures more than lovers of God; Having a form of godliness, but denying the power thereof: from such turn away. For of this sort are they which creep into houses, and lead captive silly women laden with sins, led away with divers lusts, Ever learning, and never able to come to the knowledge of the truth. (2 Timothy 3:1-7).

169

Vengeance

REPENT FROM VENGEANCE. Dearly beloved, avenge not yourselves, but rather give place unto wrath: for it is written, Vengeance is mine; I will repay, saith the Lord. Therefore if thine enemy hunger, feed him; if he thirst, give him drink: for in so doing thou shalt heap coals of fire on his head. Be not overcome of evil, but overcome evil with good. (Romans 12:19-21).

170

Wickedness

REPENT FROM WICKEDNESS. The proverbs of Solomon. A wise son maketh a glad father: but a foolish son is the heaviness of his mother. Treasures of wickedness profit nothing: but righteousness delivereth from death. The Lord will not suffer the soul of the righteous to famish: but he casteth away the substance of the wicked. He becometh poor that dealeth with a slack hand: but the hand of the diligent maketh rich. He that gathereth in summer is a wise son: but he that sleepeth in harvest is a son that causeth shame. Blessings are upon the head of the just: but violence covereth the mouth of the wicked. The memory of the just is blessed: but the name of the wicked shall rot. (Proverbs 10:1-7).

171

Worldliness

REPENT FROM WORLDLINESS. I have given them thy word; and the world hath hated them, because they are not of the world, even as I am not of the world. I pray not that thou shouldest take them out of the world, but that thou shouldest keep them from the evil. They are not of the world, even as I am not of the world. Sanctify them through thy truth: thy word is truth. As thou hast sent me into the world, even so have I also sent them into the world. And for their sakes I sanctify myself, that they also might be sanctified through the truth. (John 17:14-19).

We want to hear from you. Please send your comments about this book to:

overcomingarthritis@hotmail.com